HEALING WITH CRYSTALS

by Pamela Chase
and
Jonathan Pawlik

Coleman Publishing
99 Milbar Boulevard
Farmingdale, New York 11735

First printing November, 1986
Manufactured in the United States of America
Cover design by Coleman Publishing

ISBN 0-87418-155-0

CONTENTS

Preface

Acknowledgments

ACKNOWLEDGMENTS

We lovingly acknowledge and thank Katryn LaVanture for her illustrations, typing and proofreading, Karen Williams for her contributions and loving support, Barb Bell for her typewriter, our friends who have shared their crystal experiences and their love with us, and finally the crystals who have patiently taught us so much.

PREFACE

Jonathan is a "stone person." "Stone people" often had rock collections when they were children, and love to browse on beaches collecting shells and beautiful pebbles. They may carry stones in their pockets and love to examine intently the rocky beds of stream bottoms. Their eyes light up if you show them your precious gem jewelry, which they may collect also. Books about crystals and gems that excited Jonathan's interest in metaphysical directions, gave a focus to an interest and love of minerals that has always been there.

I, on the other hand, am a "plant person," and I have learned a lot about crystals from Jonathan. In the beginning it was hard for me to sense the energies of crystals. Jonathan would hand me a crystal and say, "Do you sense that quiet energy?" and I would mutter, "I don't feel anything," and frustration would build up inside. Gradually, with Jonathan's loving patience, I learned how to sense subtle energies, with the crystals being catalysts in that process. The book describes our growth with crystals and the ways that we personalized our relationship with crystals.

***Healing With Crystals** is also about healing. My search for understanding and peace of mind has been through the heart, with years of therapy, peer counseling, and general intense living. The fruits of all that work seem to be a way of understanding healing which can be shared with others.*

Our marriage has been about healing also, and this book is born from a merging of our creative energies and a desire to be of service to others. Its writing has been a process where Jonathan would receive channeling and we would then integrate the material, along with other bits of information, into the healing and counseling work that we do.

The material in quotes which is not footnoted has been channeled through Jonathan from the crystal devas themselves, and from the guides that work with him. Each living thing has a consciousness which is also evolving, and we hope you will learn to see crystals and all other life with new eyes as you enjoy and grow with **Healing With Crystals.**

HEALING WITH CRYSTALS
by
Pamela Chase and Jonathan Pawlik

INTRODUCTION

It is no accident that people are currently drawn to quartz crystal. The earth is undergoing a massive process of transformation. It is becoming clearer to many that we can no longer treat the earth with disrespect without harming ourselves. We must understand the universal laws of Love, letting all our actions be guided for the greater Good of All. We are learning that we must see all living things as our brothers and sisters, honoring the Light which is within all things. Quartz crystal can teach us the ways plants and minerals work with us for wellbeing. They open their secrets to those who attune to them with love and reverence. And so they teach us a way of thankfulness and conscious effort, the way of the Aquarian Age.

Chapter I.
INTRODUCTION TO CRYSTALS

Current Uses of Quartz crystal in Technology

Amplifies sound in audio-visual equipment

Transmits a greater range of the light spectrum with less distortion than glass in optical lenses for precision equipment.

Focuses energy in lasers.

Transforms solar energy into electricity in photovoltaic cells.

Stores data in computers.

Communicates broadcast frequencies in radio transmitting stations.

Uses of Crystal Within the Human Electromagnetic System

Amplifies signals from the intuition, helping to increase awareness of one's own intuitive language.

Transmits whole spectrum light through the crown chakra to the human energy system.

Focuses love energy for specific healing purposes.

Transforms imbalanced electromagnetic energy so an even flow of life-giving energy is restored.

Stores thought forms which can be retrieved later through meditation.

Aids in interdimensional **communication.**

Kinds of Crystal

When we talk about quartz crystal we are referring natural quartz crystal.

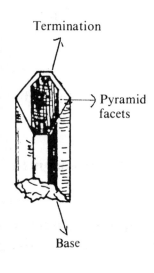

Termination

Pyramid facets

Base

Single pointed clear quartz is usually six sided with a flat base, where opposite sides are parallel. The base is often cloudy. Energy flows from the base to the **termination.** The **termination** is where the main energy transmissions come from so it is best that the **termination** and **pyramid facets** be clear and perfect. (We will use the common term "point" to refer to the **termination**.)

1a.

1b.

Clusters are single points sharing a common quartz base. Their energy is more diffuse and they can be used in a variety of ways.

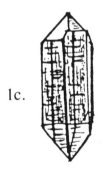

1c.

Doubly terminated crystals grow in the center of softer clay rather than out of a hard rock surface. Energy flows in two directions like a battery so these crystals are complete in themselves.

1d.

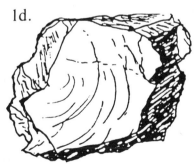

Rock crystal, most often found in Brazil, gives a more diffuse energy and is often cut and ground into different shapes such as balls.

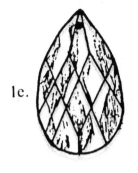

1e.

Lead crystal is a kind of glass and does not have the specific healing properties of natural clear quartz crystal.

How Quartz Crystal is Formed

Quartz is silicon dioxide tetrahedrons arranged in spiral lattices, with a hardness of 7. Silicon dioxide is a common element in the earth's crust and silicon is a common element in the human body, which partly explains the affinity quartz has with the human family.

Extremely hot water from geothermal activity dissolves silicon so that it combines with oxygen to form silicon dioxide. The process is similar to how rock candy crystals are made in a solution of sugar and very hot water.

Clear quartz crystal pockets are encased in massive white quartz veins, often in larger masses of granite. Crystal is mined on a large scale in Arkansas and Brazil.

Quartz Crystal Properties

The crystal has a highly ordered structure with an electromagnetic field that is closely attuned to the human electromagnetic field. This is because quartz and water vibrate at a similar frequency and the human body is 70 percent water.

One special property of quartz crystal is the **piezoelectric** (pronounced pie ee' zoe) effect which is caused by the particular alignment of positive and negative charges in crystal molecules. Applying mechanical pressure to a crystal will produce a measurable voltage and vice versa. In a record player for example the needle connected to a crystal element rides in the record grooves. As the needle fluctuates the mechanical stresses are converted to an electrical signal which is then amplified.

The **piezoelectric** effect properties contribute to the crystal's ability to balance the human electromagnetic energy. The tetrahedrons of silicon dioxide molecules grow in a spiral of approximately 52 degrees, the same degree as the angle between the sides and base of the Great Pyramid. This crystal structure is thought to activate the **piezoelectric** effect so that energies coming into the crystal are made more precise and balanced.

Another property of quartz is its capacity to transform a wide spectrum of light waves beyond our current vision into light that can be used by the human energy system. Thus the crystal is uniquely suited to be a tool for **communication** among people, and for understanding higher levels of reality-interdimensional communication.

Ancient Uses for Crystal

Science is only beginning to understand the unique nature of the crystal that ancients have known for centuries. American Indians, Tibetan monks, priests and kings, and shamans of every culture have used crystal as a sacred power object. Crystals have been a part of initiation rites, and used as a tool for healing and spiritual attunement.

The Atlantean civilization is said to have used crystals as antigravity devices, crystal lasers, and in different electrical devices. In the healing temples crystals were a part of the healing technology.

The pyramids of the Incan, Mayan, and Egyptian civilizations were probably created through sonic levitation and crystal laser quarrying. The pyramids helped to balance the Earth's electromagnetic energies and were used in interdimensional communication and many other purposes.

According to Edgar Cayce and other channels, crystals were misused particularly in Atlantis and so knowledge about them was "put into storage." More of this knowledge is being revealed as we move into the Aquarian Age.

Chapter II.
CARING FOR CRYSTALS

Choosing a Crystal

Choosing a crystal is a highly individual process. Each crystal has its own unique energy and some crystals will feel more "energized" than others. Also, each person's energy field is unique so people may respond to the same crystal differently. It is important to **affirm your own intuition** when choosing a crystal. People report feeling "drawn" to the same crystal repeatedly, or one crystal seems to "speak" to them in some way. Run your hand above the crystals or hold them and see which ones you "enjoy feeling." Trust your sensing and affirm that you are being drawn to the right crystals for you at this time.

In general look for clarity, especially at the point and pyramid facets, and perfect points if possible. If the point or pyramid facets are damaged in some way it can change the way energy interacts with the crystal structure, somewhat limiting the effectiveness of the crystal. All other things being equal, a larger crystal will have more power. Consider the purposes for your crystals. Smaller ones can be very effective individually programmed crystals, while larger ones can be useful in balancing energies. Crystals are like people — be sensitive and open to the unique gift each has to offer.

Storing a Crystal

Crystals like to be stored in air and sunlight, and they like to be used and enjoyed. Personal crystals can be kept in open, natural containers. If you are using a particular crystal for meditation or direct healing work, it is better not to store it in continuing sunlight so that you don't overcharge it. However, crystals whose purpose is to amplify the energies of an area love to be kept in sunlight.

If you want to protect a crystal or when carrying it, use natural fabric such as silk or cotton and make sure that the point is protected. You can use black, red, or violet material or any color that feels right to you.

If you store a crystal in the dark for a long period of time, it will need to be recharged in sunlight for optimal functioning.

Cleaning Crystals

Quartz crystals can collect various forms of negative or static energies over a period of time such as electronic pollution, negative thought forms and emotions, loud inharmonious sounds, or imbalanced electromagnetic energies. Crystals may crack or develop inclusions as they balance particularly strong imbalanced energies so be aware of this phenomenon. It is important to clean and charge a crystal when you first get it and frequently thereafter to keep it at its highest level of functioning.

Some ways to tell if a crystal needs cleaning are decreased energy coming from it, increased cloudiness within it, or stickiness to the touch. There are many ways to clean a crystal -- choose what seems most right for you.

1. For quick cleaning at the end of the day or after healing work: hold the crystal under cold running water between both hands for half a minute or so and visualize white light clearing and illuminating the crystal. Thank and love the crystal for its service.

2. Pass the crystal through sage smoke affirming that the crystal is pure and clear. Again, thank and love the crystal.

3. For a more thorough cleaning we like to place the crystals in a salt water solution for 24 to 48 hours using 1 cup sea salt, 1 cup apple cider vinegar (items purchased at the health food store) to 1 gallon spring or distilled water. Other proportions of salt to water can be used and vinegar can be omitted.

4. If a crystal is carrying a particularly strong negative influence, it can be buried underground for 2 to 7 days.

5. Crystals can also be buried in sea salt for 1 to 7 days.

We try to clean crystals thoroughly that we use often once every couple of weeks or so for best functioning.

Charging Crystals

Once crystals have been cleared of static, they must be charged with positive energies.

1. Quick charging is possible by placing them in the sun for 10 minutes or longer.

2. We like to charge crystals by placing them on a white cloth in direct sun (and moon) outside. Crystals need a minimum of 6 hours in the sun and a full day, or day and night is better.

3. If for some reason 6 hours of sunlight is not possible, we ask the devas and other spirits who channel their healing energies through the crystals to help charge and prepare them for healing use. We visualize them sparkling and clear and full of sunlight, and affirm that they are being fully charged.

4. We also charge crystals, particularly in inclement weather, by placing them on a crystal cluster for a day or two. It is particularly effective to keep pendants and crystals that you carry with you on a crystal cluster overnight after washing them so that they are optimally charged for the next day.

5. Crystals can be charged in snowstorms, thunderstorms, and other dynamic weather conditions.

6. Keeping crystals in power spots such as pyramids, mountain tops, holy places, or energy vortexes also charges them.

Crystals appreciate being treated carefully and with love. Be sensitive to their needs and they will reward you with expanding awareness.

Chapter III.
BEGINNING WORK WITH QUARTZ CRYSTALS

Familiarizing Yourself With Crystal

1. Take time to hold the crystal in the light and examine its beautiful facets. Let your imagination find the rainbows and galaxies inside your crystal. Appreciate and thank your crystal for its unique gifts. Then close your eyes and remember as many details as you can about your crystal.

2. Hold your crystal in your left (receiving) hand with the point toward your body for a minute or so. Be aware of any sensations of warmth, tingling, pressure, "electric current" sensations, or other reactions.

3. Hold your hands about four inches apart as if you were holding an imaginary ball. Now hold the crystal in your right hand with the point facing toward the left palm and draw circles in the field in front of your left palm. Be aware of the sensations.

4. Hold the crystal in your left hand, point toward your body, and then place it away from you for the same amount of time. Repeat several cycles and notice the changes.

5. Roll the crystal between your hands. Then hold it still in your left hand, point toward the body. Repeat, and notice the "piezoelectric" effect.

6. With the crystal in your right hand, touch the point to each chakra as a way of attuning yourself with it.

7. Hold the crystal in your right hand and hold the crystal in front of your third eye, point away from the forehead. Experiment to find the right distance from your forehead. Sense the energy. Now turn the crystal point toward your forehead and notice the difference.

8. Again, hold the crystal point away from your third eye and image a color. Then see the crystal being this color, concentrating on this image. Turn the crystal point toward your forehead and remain receptive. You can repeat this exercise using shapes, images, or feelings.

Meditation With Quartz Crystal

Crystal is helpful with meditation for many reasons. Because of its balancing effects it can help you reach alpha and theta states more quickly and deeply so that just holding a crystal is very relaxing. The crystal amplifies signals from your intuition, helping you to increase awareness of your own intuitive language. If you receive pictures or symbols, you may find them more vivid or prolific, something like "tuning the picture" on a TV screen. If you receive "energy sensations" and feelings, differences are more clearly perceived making it easier to "hear" and "sense" your wisdom.

The first step in working with the crystal is to attune it to your energies by holding it. There are several ways you can hold the crystal for meditation. One is to hold it in your left (receiving) hand with the point toward the fingertips. If you wish to feel the concentrated energy from the crystal you can face the point toward you.

Another way to hold it is to cup your hands, placing your left hand on the bottom and your right (sending) hand on the top. The crystal sits in your right hand with point upwards. It helps if the crystal has a flat base for this. You can also hold or tape the crystal to your third eye, point up. This position seems a little more sensitive than the others so watch for headaches, dizziness, or spaciness when the crystal is on your forehead.

It is best to work with one crystal at a time in meditation, and not to let others hold or touch your meditation crystal.

Crystals can help calm and focus any meditation practice: sitting, breathing, affirmations, visualizations, and other practices. Breathing with the crystal helps you attune with it.

You can visualize yourself "sitting in a favorite natural place. You are surrounded with a circle of crystals, points facing counterclockwise, with special ones pointing toward you at each of the four directions. You are holding a crystal point up in your cupped hands."

This visualization can help you relax and amplify your attunement with the Earth Mother. As well as holding single pointed crystals in meditation, you can keep a cluster in your special meditation place to amplify higher energies.

It can be helpful to work with a meditation for attunement:

"Become aware of how you are feeling physically, emotionally, mentally, spiritually, as you prepare to sit with your meditation crystal . . . Take a few breaths inhaling slowly, holding for a moment, then exhaling slowly . . . As you hold your crystal you may experience a variety of sensations such as temperature changes, a tingling sensation, or maybe a sense of expanding peace within yourself . . . It is good now to sit quietly in a receptive state allowing the vibrations of the crystal to harmonize with yours . . . With thoughts of pure love and light ask your crystal to open an area of its structure so that you may enter inside its perfect form . . . Observe how your crystal creates a special space for you to come within its being . . . Enter your crystal now through the doorway of light provided for you . . . Feeling in a state of perfect balance, you choose to explore the interior of your crystal . . Allow all of your senses to be open to experience your crystal . . . Touch its sides, its foundations with your hands, your face . . . Allow your body to lean against a crystal wall . . . Listen for any sounds you may hear . . . Feel the sense of being at home, being totally welcome by your crystal . . . Pause now in stillness for a few moments to allow the integration of the attunement . . . Prepare now to leave the crystal, thanking it for sharing its energies with you and return to the present."

Crystals can also help you attune to your Higher Self, guides, and entities in other realities as you learn to merge with the crystal and with your own Higher nature. When crystals focus light through a chakra the perfected state of the chakra is amplified. Thus crystals can act as a catalyst for opening the higher energy centers from the heart up. Once the crystal has helped you make a "light channel" to your Higher Self, then communication with other entities can be made through that channel of light.

If you want to open your chakras you can hold the meditation crystal and visualize crystal light illuminating each chakra. Affirm that the chakra is in its perfect harmony and flow with all other centers of the body.

It is important to be patient as you practice. Trust in your abilities to be at one with your Higher Self nature. Love yourself unconditionally, releasing fear and doubt. See yourself as a crystal-clear and filled with sparkling light, for indeed you are.

Healing with Crystals

You can amplify your own body's energies by wearing or carrying a single-pointed or doubly-terminated crystal. The crystal helps stabilize and balance physical and emotional ups and downs, and helps transform any negative energies coming in. You can visualize yourself "protected inside a large crystal, bathed in crystal light with your energy focused upward through the point where it expands into the greater Light."

A pendant will stimulate and balance your energies no matter which way the point is facing. Worn with the point down over the heart, it can ground your energies, stimulate your thymus gland, and amplify your sense of compassion. With the point up your spiritual growth can be expanded. A double-terminated crystal accomplished both tasks. A crystal worn at the throat would stimulate your thyroid gland and your creativity.

A pendant or crystal worn or carried on a daily basis needs to be cleaned often by running under cold water and affirming its purity, and charging overnight on a cluster if possible and in the sun frequently. More thorough cleanings are also necessary.

Quartz clusters love to be in a room amplifying your loving vibrations and absorbing imbalanced energies. If you have had an upset or an argument you can quick clean and charge your clusters and they will balance the negative energy and help you feel better more quickly. Shirley MacLaine in *Dancing in the Light*2 puts clusters in the four corners of her bathtub as she takes a bath. If you do healing or body work you can put clusters around your room or under your healing table.

For optimal functioning you need to have separate crystals for healing purposes from your meditation crystal, because the energies involved are different.

When working with crystals it is important to be aware of when you've had enough energy, particularly if you are in a group situation where there are a lot of crystals around. Watch for any signs of agitation or restlessness, dizziness, headaches, or spaciness. You can move away from the crystal, get some exercise, or go outside to help ground the energy. It is generally all right for others to handle your crystals for healing, use your own discretion and preferences.

Relieving Pain with Crystals

There are several ways to relieve pain with the crystal. One way is to place your left (receiving) hand on or slightly off the painful area. You may feel an energy blockage, pressure, tingling, or pain in your left hand, and there may not seem to be a flow of energy. Hold the crystal in your right (sending) hand. You can rotate your right hand in a counterclockwise circle to stimulate the energy flow. This position is particularly good for headaches.

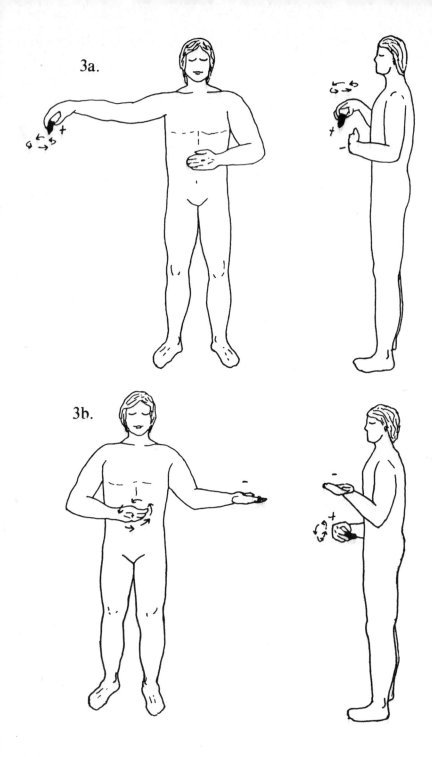

3a.

3b.

Another way is to place the crystal in your left hand with the point toward your body and your right hand on or slightly off the body, increasing the energy flow to this area as it moves from your negative hand to your positive hand. Use whichever method seems to bring the most relief. We often do a combination of both, first "drawing out" and then increasing the flow of energy to the area. The process can take anywhere from a minute to twenty minutes or so. After that time it is best to stop the crystal work, until you get a better feel for the energy and then you will have other clues to know how long to work. It is possible to place crystals directly on the body, but the way the points are facing is important. Therefore in the beginning it is best to work with the crystals in your hands. As you become more sensitive to the energies involved you can sense intuitively how to place the crystals on the body.

Giving Yourself Energy with Crystals.

When you first wake up in the morning or when you are feeling a little droopy, you can increase your energy by holding the crystal in your right hand, point toward your fingertips, and rotate the crystal counterclockwise over each chakra. Try to sense in your left hand when the chakra has had enough energy. You can start by rotating at each chakra for a half minute or so. Finish by holding the point steadily at each chakra, affirming that the chakra is open to its appropriate degree and in harmony with the other chakras.[3]

Another way to give yourself energy is to hold crystals in each hand, the left crystal pointing toward your body and the right crystal pointing away from your body. Standing or lying in the sun amplifies this energy circuit. Double-terminated crystals can be good to use for this purpose because they are a complete circuit in themselves and thus stimulate energy flow in the body.

After doing any healing work it is a good idea to wash your hands to release negative energy. You can wash the crystal at the same time!

Drinking **crystal water** increases and balances your energy also. You can make it by placing a crystal in a glass container, adding distilled or spring water, and setting it in the sun for a minimum of 6 hours. We use a gallon jar that restaurants use for mayonnaise and pickles. A glass with every meal would be plenty — more than that could cause overstimulation. You can take a glass before and after you go for a massage, chiropractic appointment, or other healing treatment to help integrate the energies. Heating or cooling the **crystal water** affects the energy, so keep it at room temperature and use discretion with it when you are taking other medications.

A method for working with absentee healing is to hold the crystal in your right hand, point toward your fingertips, and visualize the person being surrounded by crystal light. The crystal will amplify your healing affirmations and your love.

You can make a healing center by surrounding a cluster with single-pointed crystals going counterclockwise or in various other configurations. The person's picture or name goes under the cluster and the circle can be topped with a pyramid. Affirm that the person is continually surrounded with healing light. Any sacred object that you use for healing can be surrounded by crystals to amplify its energies.

Carry or wear your healing crystal to attune it to your energies, and remember to clean it often.

FOOTNOTES

[1]Taken from Randall and Vicki Baer, *Windows of Light,* (New York: Harper & Row, 1984), p. 60.

[2]Shirley MacLaine, *Dancing in the Light* (New York: Bantam Books, 1985) p. 8.

[3]Randall and Vicki Baer, *Windows of Light* (New York: Harper and Row, 1984) p. 60.

Chapter IV.
THE PENDULUM AND OTHER USES
FOR THE QUARTZ CRYSTAL

Using a Quartz Crystal Pendulum

Pendulums are an excellent tool for developing your intuition because they essentially function as a biofeedback device for contact with your Higher Self. Their best use is to help you verify the guidance you get in other ways and to teach you about listening to your Higher Self as you go about your daily life.

To begin using a crystal pendulum, carry it with you for at least 3 days to attune it to your energy. As you first hold it, experiment with the length of the chain or cord. A comfortable place will probably be between 3 and 12 inches.

Ask the pendulum to show you a "yes" or a "no." It is best to use the system that comes from your Higher Self. If you get no response you can program your pendulum. Decide on a system such as clockwise (yes) and counterclockwise (no), or vertical (yes) and horizontal (no), or a combination of these positions. Move the pendulum in your "yes" direction, visualizing YES in bold letters on your mental screen, and "connecting" it to how you see or feel the "yes" motion. Affirm that this is a "yes." Repeat with the "no" motion. Then ask your pendulum to show you a "yes" or a "no." It may take some practice over a period of time. Trust that you are learning well and persevere until you get a response.

Now you are ready to begin asking questions that can be answered "yes" or "no." When working do not have your arms or legs crossed or touching each other. It is good to wash your hands before starting. Work on an uncluttered surface, away from electrical equipment and magnets.

Ask your pendulum, "Are we in harmony?" or "Am I in tune with my pendulum?" **Readings are easily influenced by your emotional state of mind regarding the question, fatigue or illness, or any inharmonious energies present.** Learning to stay in harmony with your pendulum is one of the most challenging lessons in working with it. Approach the pendulum with an attitude like "reading the gas meter."

As you receive answers, listen to your "inner voice." Watch for other bodily sensations such as a tingling in the hands, tightening of the muscles in the back of the neck, yawning, a tic in the eyelid, or momentary numbness or dizziness. You can ask your pendulum how these signals are to be interpreted. Once you have developed your intuitive language you will no longer need to use the pendulum.

You gain additional information by noting the strength of the pendulum's responses, particularly in healing work. At some point, such as when your pendulum gives you a different response than your standard yes/no movements, it is a good idea to ask your pendulum to indicate how it would move for each of the following questions:

1. "I (pendulum) have no opinion on the question being asked."
2. "I don't want to respond to the question."
3. "You need to clarify your question and ask it in a different way."
4. "Now is not the appropriate time to ask that question."

With more experience you can create an arc with several possibilities and ask the pendulum to point to the best possibility. For example, you can make an arc for the 7 colors and ask the pendulum to point to the color you need at the time. This method is less laborious than going through each color for example, and asking a yes/no question.

Here is a list of some of the possible uses for your pendulum, of the yes/no variety:

1. colors
2. flower and gem essences, appropriate gemstones
3. vitamins, cell salts, foods
4. appropriate activities
5. appropriate times for activities
6. plant needs
7. choosing crystals
8. cleaning and charging particular crystals, general care
9. uses for particular crystals (Are you a meditation/healing crystal?)
10. appropriate affirmations or other practices to use with crystals.

We have learned a great deal about crystal from dialoguing with our pendulums and subsequent practice.

In the healing model we use, it is important to know which hand has a negative charge (receiving hand) and which hand has the positive charge (sending hand). To determine this, you can hold the pendulum over your left and then your right palm. If the charge is negative, the pendulum will rotate clockwise and this becomes your receiving hand. The pendulum rotates counterclockwise over your positive or sending hand. It is advisable to check this, particularly if you are left handed.

With a crystal pendulum, you can also infuse energy into the chakras by holding the pendulum over each chakra until it becomes still. More possibilities for using the pendulum will be discussed later.

The most important thing to remember is to use the pendulum with the highest intentions, to use it to confirm other means of intuitive guidance so that you don't become overly dependent on it, and to learn when you are in harmony with your Higher Self.

Other Uses for Quartz Crystal

1. A crystal can be put under your pillow, point up, to help you remember your dreams.

2. For better growth and health of plants, place a crystal directly adjacent to the plant with the point upward. You can water plants with crystal water and keep clusters around them. Rocks and plants benefit each other.

3. Sometimes you can quiet a screaming baby by giving him or her a crystal to hold.

4. Animals respond well to crystals in their environment and crystal work in general when they are ill.

5. You can recharge weak (not dead) batteries by putting them on clusters.

6. In general crystals can help amplify the energy in any electrical device. Use your inventiveness and creativity here!

Crystals teach us through their proper use to honor all of nature, and to honor ourselves as well, as co-creators of our universe. When we act clearly and with love in our hearts, crystals give us their gift of helping us merge with the greater Truth and Light.

Chapter V.
PROGRAMMING YOUR CRYSTALS

Programming Crystals

Programming a crystal is a way of co-creating that can effect powerful changes as you continue to use the crystal. The crystal amplifies the program and continues to emit the energy, something like a tape recorder. One of my own more graphic experiences has been in working to remember my dreams. When I put a crystal under my pillow and affirmed that I would remember my dreams in the morning, I did indeed remember more of them. When I programmed the crystal to amplify my dreams so that I could recall them in the morning, the dreams were even more complete and also more vivid.

A crystal becomes programmed with your intention when you use it repeatedly for a specific purpose such as meditation or healing. This is the simplest type of programming. When you want a crystal to retain a program over a period of time it is more effective to program the crystal consciously. You can put more than one program into a crystal but the programs need to be compatible. You need to wait a few days before adding a program so that the crystal can attune with the energy.

Types of Crystals to be Programmed

All crystals have a higher purpose to serve. Some crystals are better for meditation, some for healing, and some are here as "instructors" for us. These crystals already have data stored within them. Therefore it is a good idea to ask your Higher Self either through a crystal pendulum or through direct contact whether there are any programs stored presently within your crystal. If there are, then you would probably not want to program this crystal. Instead, you would work with it according to its highest purpose.

The next step might be to use your pendulum or contact your Higher Self to "fine tune" the best uses or programs for your particular crystal.

Preparing for Programming

Spend some time with a pencil and paper writing a concise, potent affirmation that is for the "highest good of all concerned." Attune with your crystal visually, sensing the perfection of its form. You may want to touch the crystal to your chakras — do whatever helps you to best attune to it. You can hold the main facet of the crystal to your third eye and find the place where you connect most intensely with your crystal.

Programming Steps

There are many ways to program a crystal. Here are the steps we follow — again, do what seems intuitively best for you.

1. Place your hands in your lap, with the right (sending) hand cupped inside your left hand, with the crystal in the right palm, point toward your fingertips.

2. **Attune** with the crystal, sensing the energy coming from it and visualizing a pure white light bridge connecting you with your crystal. Say to your crystal, "I merge my being with you," and sense your integration with it.

3. Ask your crystal to **open a part of its matrix** to receive the program. You can visualize an area of light opening inside the crystal, again with appreciation for the crystal. Give your crystal time and let your intuitive awareness guide you as to when this is done. (Normally a minute or two is all that is needed.)

4. At this point, if you are programming color, sound, the vibrations of a place, or other information over a period of time, you can place the crystal on the speaker etc. and leave it. Follow your intuitive guidance about the amount of time needed. Then move to step 7, protecting your crystal with Light.

5. For a thought program you can raise the crystal to your third eye and **repeat your affirmation** three or more times. Lower the crystal to your lap and continue your visualization and affirmations.

6. Focus your awareness on your breath and **breathe** your affirmations and your love into the crystal.

7. **Affirm a protection** of pure white light around your crystal. "I surround you with the white light of love and protection," thanking your crystal for its service.

You are the only person who can take out a program that you have put into the crystal. **Cleaning and charging does not erase a program, conscious intent does.** To take a program out of a crystal, just follow the same process you used to enter the program, telling your crystal that you are focusing pure white light to erase that existing program.

Keep in mind the qualities of trust and patience as you unfold co-creatively with the mineral kingdom. Always honor the sacred space that is present within you as well as the crystal. Love and nurture your crystal and the crystal will respond in kind to you.

Programming Crystals in Meditation

When you work with meditation, you usually work in one of two modes. One mode is a more active, searching communication with the Higher Self, and usually involves a practice such as chanting a mantra or working with a visualization. A more receptive mode involves becoming a silent observer or listener to hear what is being shared with you. Often in a meditation sitting you may do both. A **meditation** crystal is a more broadly focused crystal that can be programmed for both modes to facilitate particular needs. With this crystal you can develop your own unique meditation program that helps you "become quiet within" by adding a number of compatible programs such as the following possibilities:

1. Music or sound that uplifts or centers you such as a Beethoven symphony or the sound of a stream, is excellent. Crystals work particularly well with amplifying the healing qualities of sound.

2. Tone your "soul tone" into the crystal.

3. Enter chants and mantras.

4. Work with specific affirmations such as:
   a. I am relaxed, focused, and center in Love.
   b. I am merging with the Light.

5. Take this crystal to sacred places and energy vortex spots and program the crystal to receive their energies.

6. Put into the crystal specific power symbols from other cultures that have meaning for you, such as the "om" or "yin-yang" symbols.

A more specialized kind of meditation crystal would be one programmed with the **energies of a particular master.** First you would merge your consciousness and your total essence with the energy essence of the master.

1. Read to your crystal words that have been written by the master.

2. Repeatedly write his or her name on paper, while holding the crystal, and leave the crystal on the paper.

3. Work with pictures or photographs, leaving the crystal on them for a period of time.

4. Project or visualize the energy from a sacred place or object relating to the master. Pure intent and pure love are essential in this process.

Another more specialized kind of crystal is the **Higher Self attunement** crystal. This crystal is more singularly focused for the purpose of becoming more attuned to the Divine Will in relationship to your own will, and is used in the receptive mode.

1. For the initial program, work with a specific affirmation such as "My connection with my Higher Self is expanding and becoming clearer."

You will find that many times the information received as you work receptively will clarify the initial program. Once the bridge to the Higher Self has been connected then it is possible for different kinds of interdimensional communication to travel the light path . . .

Programming Crystals for Healing

In general, we program healing crystals to "not absorb imbalanced energy," especially if they will be used on the body, or held. We find that crystals with this program may need to be cleaned less frequently. This is a good program for crystals that you are using daily, and serves as a protection for the crystal.

These are suggestions for other programs to use with healing crystals, particularly with crystals you might place on the body.

Crystals for physical healing.

1. "You surround me with Light and protection for my highest good," can be a good affirmation for a crystal that you wear or carry.

2. For healing a specific area of the body, you can visualize the area perfectly healed and project this image into the crystal, affirming your physical wholeness and perfection with love and confidence.

3. In energy balancing work we use crystals with the following program with areas of blocked energy. "You are drawing out the optimal quantity of imbalanced energies at this time without absorbing any imbalanced energies."

4. To expand the energies for healing and balance: "You are a pure channel for cosmic vibrations for consciousness expansion, without absorbing imbalanced energies."

5. Our grid crystals are programmed: "You are continuously receiving and transmitting unconditional love (without absorbing imbalanced energies)."

6. Use a separate crystal for each chakra to open, balance, and expand that chakra.

7. Color programmed crystals are useful for balancing and expanding the life force in the chakras, particularly for physical balance. After opening the matrix, place them under colored filters, a day on each side, in the sun.

Crystals for emotional/mental healing

In general you might hold these crystals while working with specific issues, or you could wear or carry them with you as you work with affirmations during the day. It is important to keep them cleaned and charged. The crystals also appreciate being protected with the protection phrase "without absorbing imbalanced energies." There are some verbal and nonverbal ways you can program these crystals, as well as suggestions for some specific healing purposes, such as past life work.

1. Use music that represents for you the qualities of courage, patience, or resonates with affirmations you plan to use.

2. Here are examples of affirmations:

    a. I, crystal, am a catalyst for bringing blocked energies into conscious awareness for release.

    b. You are filled with forgiveness, releasing stored memories that block the flow of forgiveness.

    c. I am being all that I am.

    d. I radiate love to all creation.

    e. The divine plan of my life is unfolding in peace and harmony.

    f. Just be.

3. Crystals can be used to link directly into the subconscious mind where **past life experiences** are stored. It is very important for your intentions to be pure before entering into this co-creative capacity with the crystal.

   a. A good program would be "You are accessing past lifetimes for lessons that can best be integrated at this time for my growth and highest good (without absorbing imbalanced energies)."

   b. A related program would be "You are accessing past lifetimes that can become sources of strength, courage, and further connection with my Higher Self to help me in this lifetime."

If you are guiding another person in a past life regression it can be helpful to have 2 programmed crystals, one for each of you. This is so your attunement to the person being regressed is deepened.

4. Crystals can also be used to **see into the future.** If you have apprehensions about this particular process then it is best left alone.

   a. An affirmation you would use would be "Show me key elements that are ahead of me in this lifetime that I can now utilize so that I can truly achieve the highest purpose for my soul in this life." Also include a protection for this crystal.

Other Types of Programs

Crystals have a powerful capacity for storing symbols, archetypes, and systems of thought that you can use to help you learn more about that information. In general you follow the steps for programming, opening the matrix, and then you program the crystal to store and amplify the particular information, placing the crystal on the information.

1. For example, you can place a crystal on a **tarot** deck, or on a specific card, to help you deepen your understanding of particular cards and of the system itself.

2. In **astrology** you can use the crystal to better understand the symbolism and power of your key planetary configurations. The crystal would also amplify the positive effects of those energy forms for your highest good. For example, if you wanted to understand and amplify the effects of a grand trine in your chart, write down the particular symbols that are involved, and draw the triangle on paper. Visualize and affirm that the energy of the configuration is assimilated within the structure of the crystal. You can also do this with **transits** and then take the program out once the transit has passed.

"Every crystal has a particular function in life and can gravitate to even greater levels of service and responsibility through the conscious and subconscious energies emerging from the human kingdom. Whenever the crystal receives a visual imprint into its being, the pictures are not only stored within but amplified geometrically each time that image is called for from the crystal in a meditation. Greater insights will emerge as you gain a greater awareness of the possibilities of the crystal to work with you."

Chapter VI.
HEALING WITH CRYSTALS

Healing — An Overview

Healing can be viewed as a three step process involving clearing out blockages that impede growth, infusing with positive healing energies, and spiritually expanding into new understandings.

We live in a sea of energy called "life force" energy. Hindus call it "prana" and the Chinese call it "chi." It is said to originate from the sun, and has been linked to negatively charged ions. In addition, "prana" or "chi" seems to be imbued with qualities of love, compassion, joy, and vitality, so that when we are optimally healthy this energy flows through us like water, constantly renewing us on physical, emotional, mental, and spiritual levels. When we breathe deeply of "prana" or "chi" we renew our bodies physically, and when we visualize or are receptive to the life giving qualities of this energy we are renewed spiritually as well.

Holistic systems of healing recognize that conflicts in beliefs manifest as emotional/mental imbalances and physical imbalances — pain and disease. All thoughts are energy and our positive thoughts move in a flowing, changing manner, in tune with the life force energy. Repetitive negative thoughts can cause an energy blockage, a build-up of positive ions, resulting in a restricted flow of "life force energy." We often hold onto negative thoughts because of the mistaken belief that if we examine the negativity we will recreate the pain and be forever stuck in it. And so we block the thought and the feelings that went with it from our conscious memories. This "package" is stored in our subconscious, our energy fields, and in our physical bodies. Energy flow in other parts of the body can thus be altered and we feel "out of balance."

To strengthen your skills at sensing blocked energy, hold your receiving hand over an area of your body that has been recently injured, or that is sore or very tight. You may feel a lack of energy flow, pain, pressure, or "uncomfortableness" in your hand. If this blockage is not cleared, toxic wastes can build up and cells do not function optimally, resulting in physical disease.

Ultimately what heals a negative thought pattern or a conflict in beliefs is being able to love and accept oneself. It is possible to find the hurting places inside ourselves, and to give that part of us the compassion which can heal the pain. When we can build our own confidence, inner peace, and self-acceptance, it is possible to forgive and accept others as well.

When you work with others you hold in your mind their perfection of body, mind, and spirit, seeing yourself as a channel for light, unconditional love, and eternal peace. When you do this you surround the person with the life force energy of compassion, which acts as a catalyst for him or her to heal a negative thought pattern.

This model of healing involves becoming aware of and **clearing** negative thoughts in the mind using visualization, release of the emotions involved, and clearing the blockages in the energy field itself — the first step. This is an important step because it is the mind that controls the energy flow. A moment of awareness and loving release can clear the energy field, and the difference in how you feel is noticeable.

Once the blockages are cleared, the next step is to **infuse** energy into specific areas so that the electromagnetic field is balanced, and energies are flowing evenly once again. This is done with positive, affirming thoughts and visualizations, and an attitude of compassion and nurturing. An example of this infusion would be visualizing an area of the body totally healed and affirming that we are totally healthy, totally loved, and filled with vital life energy like rivers of light. Work is also done with the electromagnetic field to infuse energy in specific areas, balance each chakra and move energies evenly through the field.

The final step is to **contact and be receptive to the Higher Self** through visualization and attunement. Chakras can be expanded and the electromagnetic field energies can be heightened for increased spiritual awareness.

Crystals as amplifiers of thought can be helpful in all three stages of attitudinal healing, and crystals are used in various ways to work with the energy field healing.

Because your physical body is an excellent personal biofeedback tool, it is valuable to work with yourself with crystal before working with others. You can pick a crystal to work with one of your chakras, and program it to amplify and balance the chakra energies. The heart chakra can be a good first choice because the heart chakra relates to self-acceptance. The following section describes ways of thinking about and working with the chakras.

A next step might be to use a hand-held generator crystal for self-healing, which is described in the self-healing section. There are also ideas for programming crystals to use in self-healing meditations.

Vital life force energies enter the electromagnetic system primarily through three areas — the feet, the hands, and through the head at the base of the skull and at the top of the head. Crystals can be used at these areas to draw out blocked energies or to infuse energies. Subsequent sections include ways of working with crystals in grid patterns, ideas for programming crystals for healing, and a format that we use in a crystal energy balancing session. **Above all it is important for you to find your own ways of working with crystals.** Let these ideas be seed thoughts to get you started and excite you with further possibilities.

The Chakras

The chakras can be balanced and amplified through thought and energy field work with crystals. The word chakra comes from the Sanskrit meaning "wheels of light," which is what they look like when photographed with Kirlian photography. The chakras are points of entry and also transducers for life force energies. Every chakra when balanced reflects a particular pattern of energy that can be sensed as color or a "sense perception." Likewise, when the chakra is blocked, the imbalance is reflected as a different color or "sense perception." The chakras are like windows in the houses that are our bodies. If the windows are small or dirty, or we close the curtains, less light can come in, and bright sunlight might be a dingy yellow color inside the house. The degree to which the chakras open to receive life force energy depends on our will, belief systems, and emotional state.

The chakras stimulate the endocrine glands which then secrete hormones for cell growth and maintenance. If an endocrine gland does not receive enough life force energy, cells do not function properly, resulting in pain or dis-ease. Pain and illness are messages that thoughts are in some way blocking the flow of life force energy.

When an imbalance is present in a particular chakra, the key to restoring harmony and flow also lies within the area of development represented by the chakra. For example, if we find it difficult to express our needs, our truth, or our creativity, resulting in restricted flow in the throat chakra, we can sing. Singing can keep the throat chakra in better balance and also uplift the spirit as well. By monitoring the energy flow in the chakras we can receive feedback on beliefs that give us physical vitality, peace of mind, and the strengthened intuitive awareness that comes from being connected to the Source of all life.

The book **Transformers, the Therapists of the Future** by Jacqueline Small (DeVorss and Company, Box 550, Marina del Ray, Ca. 90294, 1982) gives an excellent description of the growth process through the chakras, from which some of these ideas are taken.

Root Chakra

The root chakra represents our will to live and our physical vitality. The color red is associated with this chakra because red is a vibration of courage as well as physical vitality. This is a level of physical mastery of our bodies as well as mastery of our physical survival in the outer world.

When the root chakra is blocked, we may be perceiving the world as threatening or unsafe. If we have deep-rooted beliefs that we don't deserve to live or don't want to live, we may block the life force at this level. Trusting the universe to supply our abundance and prosperity can help balance the root chakra.

1. Meaning: will to live — joy in everyday physical existence

2. Color: red

3. Endocrine glands: gonads

4. Affirmation: I live courageously, honoring the natural vitality of my physical body.

5. Location: base of spine, pubic bone

Spleen or Lower Abdomen Chakra

This chakra has to do with processing basic emotional sensations of anger and fear, love and trust as we relate to other people. Here we assimilate feelings and let go of that which we don't need. This chakra is also involved with self-gratification in relation to others — assimilating the pleasures of the senses in attunement with our highest good. Orange gives the qualities of hope, confidence, and understanding needed to balance this chakra.

An imbalance in this chakra can indicate several kinds of negative beliefs. Sometimes anger held in the abdominal region is a refusal to assimilate new understandings and to let go of the grievances. A blockage here can also mean a denial of any feelings such as rightful anger, or love and compassion described by the belief that "Only weak people express their feelings. Strong people don't cry."

Another difficulty that can manifest in this area is overgratification of the senses coming from a belief that "There is not enough love for me in this world. I am not enough, so I am seeing love in the form of pleasure." And so we overeat, oversex, and try to fill what we have defined as an emptiness.

1. Meaning: right feeling — assimilating and letting go of our feelings and sensations in healthy ways.

2. Color: orange

3. Endocrine glands: spleen, liver, pancreas, gonads

4. Affirmation: I assimilate right understanding through my feelings and senses.

5. Location: two inches below the navel

Solar Plexus Chakra

The solar plexus chakra relates to our sense of personal identity and personal power. We use our minds to construct our values and build a sense of who we are, establishing a base of personal power. Yellow is the color of mental understanding and joy that comes from building the self-concept associated with this chakra.

Imbalances in this chakra often have to do with believing that we are powerless to change a particular circumstance. Lack of self-confidence can manifest as trying to fill our stomachs with love and nurturing from the outside that we need to give to ourselves. Self doubts give rise to "butterflies in the stomach," or the belief that we don't deserve good things in life.

1. Meaning: right knowing — developing our self-confidence and trusting our abilities and values.

2. Color: yellow

3. Endocrine gland: adrenals

4. Affirmation: I own my strength and power

5. Location: two inches above the navel

Heart Chakra

We learn true self-acceptance in our hearts. The heart is self-acceptance, a non-judgmental attitude toward ourselves, that allows us to transcend where we are at any given time. Developing a sense of compassion for others teaches us to love ourselves. Green is the color of harmony and emotional balance, the qualities of compassion in action, so it is an appropriate color for the heart.

An imbalance in the heart often indicates an overly judgmental attitude towards ourselves which is sometimes projected onto others. The forgiveness that needs to occur in the heart is self-forgiveness. A heart imbalance can also indicate sadness and grief in dealing with the loss of a loved one.

1. Meaning: developing compassion for all, especially ourselves

2. Color: green

3. Endocrine gland: thymus

4. Affirmation: I accept myself fully as I am.

5. Location: heart

Throat Chakra

The throat chakra represents expressing our knowledge and our creativity according to our own unique gifts. Here is where we speak our truth and where we sing our songs for others. Blue brings mental peace and, as the color of the sky, blue is an expression of our aspirations.

A blocked throat chakra often means that we haven't said something we need to say, or that we need to be creative in some way. Sometimes there is a need to express true feelings that get clogged in the throat. Active expression of knowledge is a key here.

1. Meaning: right knowing — speaking our truth

2. Color: blue

3. Endocrine gland: thyroid

4. Affirmation: I express my truth creatively.

5. Location: throat

Third Eye Chakra

The third eye is the seat of the intuition where our empathy with others helps us receive information from our Higher Selves. Intuition feels like a calm sense of rightness, even underneath pain. Intuitive knowing also comes in many forms such as colors, symbols, sounds, pictures, an "ordinary thought," or a feeling or sense impression. Indigo, the color of the twilight sky, is the color of combined love and wisdom. These qualities combined, strengthen our intuitive abilities.

An imbalance in the third eye can indicate mental thoughts that are blocking our intuitive knowing — trying to figure something out rationally without connecting with our own loving self-acceptance.

1. Meaning: right feeling — intuitive understanding

2. Color: indigo

3. Endocrine gland: pituitary

4. Affirmation: My empathy with others strengthens my intuition.

5. Location: brow

Crown Chakra

The crown chakra is where we sense our unity with all life and act in attunement with our intuitive wisdom. Violet is a color of purification and we can visualize a violet flame at each chakra, purifying our identity at each level. At the crown chakra, violet is a color of transformation and transcendence, the qualities that bring us new kinds of awareness and understanding.

An imbalance at the crown chakra often means that we do not wish to receive guidance from our Higher Selves at that moment. We are holding onto some belief that is familiar even if it is painful. Often, moving to a new level of integration involves a little death of some part of us and there are times we hold on from fear of the unknown, blocking the love and safety that flows into us at the crown chakra.

1. Meaning: right action — sensing the unity of all life and acting on that knowledge.

2. Color: violet, purple

3. Endocrine gland: pineal

4. Affirmation: I act in total harmony with my higher wisdom.

5. Location: top of the head

When you sense imbalances in particular chakras you can use your understanding of their nature and function to help yourself and others clear the negative beliefs. During the clearing and affirmation process you can monitor the energy flow in the chakras and receive feedback on what gives optimal balance.

Self Healing — Crystal Possibilities

1. Meditation crystals that are programmed for specific purposes (suggestions follow).

2. Hand held healing crystal

3. Crystals for a specific grid (see section on grids)

4. Crystals for each chakra that are programmed to bring balance and expansion to the particular chakra without absorbing any imbalanced energies. If you plan to work with others in healing, you would need a personal set separate from those used in working with others.

Self Healing with the 3 Step Process
(see page 20)

What follows are possible uses for crystals as you work with your thoughts for healing. You can follow these steps in order, or omit some steps according to your own preferences.

Step 1 — Clearing or Drawing Out

The following steps involve the possible use of one crystal:

1. Hold a meditation crystal that is programmed to bring up thought energy that needs releasing in your receiving hand, with the point toward the body. You can also program this crystal with music that is cathartic for you. If you have a crystal programmed to help you remember your dreams, you can also use it for this process, to help you become aware of what needs to be cleared from your subconscious.

2. You can use the following visualization or a similar process to contact your subconscious to increase your awareness about what needs to be cleared:

> "Go to your favorite beautiful outdoor place ... It is a beautiful sunny day with puffy clouds floating by ... The sun is warm on your face and the breeze is pleasant and soothing ... Observe this place with all your senses and feel

the safety and peace here for you . . . Find a natural object here that appeals to you . . . Become tiny and enter it, exploring its textures, fragrances, sounds . . . While here ask your subconscious to give you a visual picture, sense impression, symbol, or feeling about what needs to be released . . . Ask from what area of the body the clearing needs to take place . . . Ask any other parts of your body to speak to you . . . Wait receptively and openly, knowing that you are totally safe . . . When you have received your message, come out of the natural object and sit once again in your beautiful place, visualizing the violet flame of purification, or streams of water or light cleansing and purifying you . . . Infuse your clearing element with the quality you are now affirming, such as patience or compassion . . . Let go . . .

3. Using a healing crystal that has been programmed to restore balance without absorbing any imbalanced energies, follow the drawing out procedure. Hold your receiving hand over any imbalanced area, and hold the crystal in your sending hand, point toward the fingertips, and rotate it counterclockwise in the air, point out or downward. Rotate until you feel the energy beginning to flow again, or a sense of calm or release of pressure, in your receiving hand. It is important to work no longer than about 10

minutes total with the drawing out process. If the blockage isn't totally released, be patient with yourself and know that you have done all that you can for now.

If you wish to use more crystals you can combine these steps with the above suggestions. Begin by:

1. Sitting in a crystal grid of 3 or 6 crystals with the points facing out during the clearing. (See section on grids)

2. You can lie down and place your programmed chakra crystals on their respective chakras, points toward the feet, and clear any chakras needed. This can be done with or without drawing out. To clear imbalanced physical or emotional energy, visualize yourself standing under a waterfall, feeling each chakra beginning with the crown being cleansed and purified. You can also use the image of the violet flame transforming any imbalanced energy at each chakra. Work with each chakra as long as you need to until you feel cleansed and light filled.

Step 2 — Infusing Energy for Healing

1. Hold a meditation crystal in your receiving hand, point toward the body, that has been programmed for self-empowerment, optimal health, or particular qualities that you are affirming.

2. Work with specific affirmations that counteract the negative thoughts, and energize these affirmations with the feelings of courage, compassion, and trust. Visualize the areas of your body or psyche as perfectly healthy, whole, and happy.

3. Hold a healing crystal in your sending hand, point toward the fingertips, and rotate counterclockwise over the specific area and then over your chakras, beginning with the root chakra, until the energy in your hands "evens out." If the area needs energy you may feel a lot of activity — tingling, heat, or pressure in your receiving hand, which is held palm up. Watch for a calming or mellowing of these senstions and a sense that the area has had enough energy. Then hold the crystal steady to "close" the chakra at the optimal level for grounding, and then move to the next chakra. Be sure to infuse the energy into each area where you've "drawn out."

4. Sit inside a grid with the points turned in towards you.

5. If you are working with the programmed chakra crystals, place them on the body with their points up toward the head, and infuse the energy in each chakra with your hand held healing crystal. You can visualize appropriate colors or affirmations for each chakra, or visualize the crystal as a perfect form, or white light at each chakra.

Step 3 — Spiritual Expansion

1. Hold or place on the third eye a meditation crystal that is programmed for connection with your Higher Self, interdimensional communication, or other meditation work and be receptive to its energies.

2. You can remain in a grid and visualize its perfect form, (triangle, Star of David) and the qualities it represents.

3. If you are working with the programmed chakra crystals, affirm that each of your chakras is "opening to the highest level in harmony and balance with your other chakras, for your higher good." Be receptive to the energies of the crystals.

4. You can hold a crystal in each hand to complete a circuit. The crystal in the receiving hand points in toward the body, and the one in the sending hand points out toward the fingertips.

Some version of self-healing is a good practice when you first wake up and when you go to bed. You will start your day feeling more balanced, refreshed, and energetic.

Placing Crystals on the Body for Self-Healing

It is possible to place crystals on the body for self-healing while sleeping, keeping several guidelines in mind. First of all, it is best to work with a mental clearing process, so that releasing old beliefs can help facilitate the healing process. It can be helpful to place a healing crystal over an area of the body where surgery has been performed, or where you have a cut, bruise, rash, etc. In general, if the area is at or below the solar plexus chakra you can point the crystal toward the feet, visualizing clearing taking place through the feet. If the area is at the heart or above, you can point the crystal toward the crown chakra. This is not a hard and fast rule, and you can point the crystal whichever way you plan to visualize the clearing process. Do not hesitate to change the directional flow of the crystal as conditions change in your energy field.

6a.

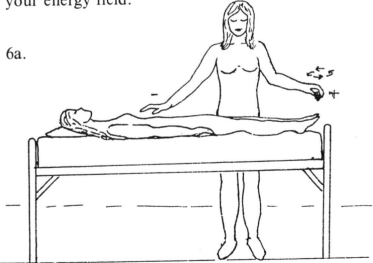

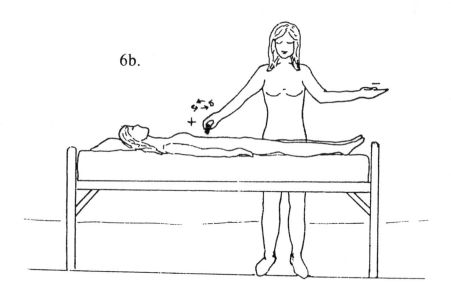

6b.

The other guideline to be aware of is overstimulation of your electromagnetic energy fields which can disrupt your sleep. Watch for jittery feelings, spontaneous jerking or twitching, or a build-up of stress in the particular area. If you feel these symptoms, try laying the crystal aside and allowing the body time to assimilate the life force energies. No two people are alike in these matters, and your beliefs about the process also influence your electromagnetic energy. Experiment and observe yourself carefully and you will find the best ways for you to keep your energy at optimal levels.

Crystal Healing with Others
(see illustrations pp. 61, 62)

It is important to understand in working with others that you are a catalyst or helper, for ultimately we heal ourselves. You can enhance the optimal flow of energy within someone else, but it is the thoughts coming from their subconscious, conscious, and superconscious levels that ultimately control the flow of energy. When the client works with visualizations and intuitive processes for clearing, self-affirmation, and greater spiritual attunement, he or she gains a greater sense of power in controlling the attitudes necessary for healing, as well as skill in using his or her own intuition for guidance. You can moniter the energy flow and assist by providing an environment with crystals (and your thoughts) that allows for optimal balancing of energies at a given point in time. There are a number of ways you can use crystals to build and amplify your own healing work.

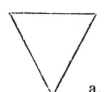 a.  b. 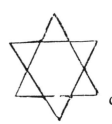 c.

Balancing the Electromagnetic Field — Crystal Grids for Healing

Perhaps one of the most powerful ways crystals can be used is in the creation of energy vortexes that amplify "healing forms" and also our own compassion and attunement with the client. These are called **grids.** Grids maintain a steady flow of energy that merge with the energy of the client. Using grids is one way that those of you who are healing practitioners of other disciplines can amplify the healing energies inherent in your systems.

In sacred geometry we learn that shapes have specific properties. The **triangle** is a 3 vibration, giving synthesis and harmony. The 6 pointed **Star of David** (figure c) is a shape of harmony, balance, and equilibrium. The inverted triangle (figure a) represents bringing the perfection of spirit into matter, and the upright triangle (figure b) symbolizes the growth of matter towards spirit. Thus these interlocking triangles represent the perfection of humanity and the balance of all creation. By visualizing and attuning to the Star of David and placing crystals in this arrangement, an energy vortex is created that amplifies balance, harmony, and the perfection of our being. You can use the principle of a grid in a variety of ways according to your own inclinations.

1. We use a **Star of David** grid of 6 single-pointed crystals sitting on top of pedestals (made with dowels and wood slabs) at table height and surrounding the healing table. Other possibilities are to install wall shelves for these crystals, thus creating a powerful field of harmony and balance.

   Connect these crystals in your mind and with a crystal before beginning each session. Clusters can also be used for a more diffuse field.

2. A double Star of David (12 crystals) that ends up looking like a clock is also a very powerful healing grid.

3. Another set of 12 crystals that we use (12 point grid) consists of 5 pairs of crystals placed at the joints, on the table, surrounding the body. Crystals or clusters are placed on each side of the neck, shoulders, hips, knees, and ankles. Crystals that direct the flow of energy are placed at the head and feet. Major joints are "intersections" of the life force and can become congested, so that crystals or clusters at the joints help clear blockages or infuse energy into the body.

   As a general rule, the directional crystals above the head and between the feet are pointed downward from head to feet as clearing and grounding take place, "to bring spirit into matter." During the infusion and expansion process the crystals are pointing upward from the feet toward the head, "to expand matter toward spirit," so that a state of perfect balance is achieved.

4. Crystal clusters can be placed on the floor underneath the healing table.

5. Also, as a general amplification of power, single-pointed crystals can be placed in the four corners of the room to move the static energy that can collect there.

6. In **Exploring Atlantis Vol. II** Rev. Dr. Frank Alper describes grids for specific physical ailments using crystal clusters. For more information write Arizona Metaphysical Society, 3639 East Claredon Road, Phoenix, Arizona 85018.

Crystal Possibilities for Programming

1. Earlier we mentioned that crystals can be programmed for the balance and expansion of each chakra.

2. Program crystals that "draw out the optimal quantity of imbalanced energies for this time without absorbing any imbalanced energies." These crystals can be placed on key chakras in grids of 3 or 6, points facing out or down toward the feet. (See illustration).

3. "Consciousness expansion" crystals are programmed "to be pure channels for cosmic vibrations that expand consciousness." They can be used also in grids of 3 or 6 on areas where you've cleared imbalances, or where energy infusion is needed. Points face in and toward the head.

4. Color can be programmed into crystals, and are best used on an appropriate chakra or area for infusing energy into that area.

5. Crystals programmed with music or personal healing tones can be used both on the body and held by the client.

6. Qualities such as forgiveness, courage, and joy can be programmed into crystals that are held by the client in the receiving hand.

7. It is important that you place within the crystals a program of protection as well as a program that they will not internalize within their structure any lingering imbalanced energies from the person.

Other Crystal Possibilities

1. Doubly-terminated crystals can be used as connectors between the chakras.

2. A crystal pendulum works well to infuse color, a tone, or energy into a chakra. You may have already noticed that when you first hold a crystal it feels very active as it releases energy to balance your system. Then the crystal seems to become "quieter." In the same way the pendulum responds through movement to correct an imbalance.
Hold the pendulum over the chakra. If it rotates, the area needs energy. Hold the pendulum in your sending hand, until it stops rotating and becomes still. It is best to have a pendulum that you use specifically for this purpose, so that it is cleaned and charged when you need it. You can amplify the energy by holding a doubly-terminated crystal in your receiving hand, and the pendulum in your sending hand. This is another simple, effective method for balancing the chakras.

3. Small clusters can be placed on specific chakras or other areas of the body for drawing out purposes.

4. If you practice other systems of healing, crystals can be taped to the top of the hands, points facing toward the fingertips, to amplify the flow of energy coming through your hands.

6c.

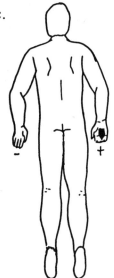

6d.

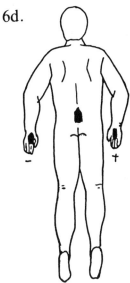

6e.

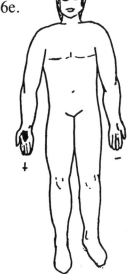

6f.

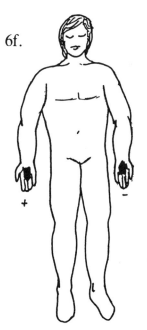

Steps in Healing — Level 1

To begin working with crystal healing, it is helpful to have a hand-held crystal, a crystal for the base of the spine, and crystals for the client to hold, to amplify the energy flows.

1. **Preparation for Healing:**

   a. Take crystal water, flower, or gem essences.

   b. Center yourself and affirm that your work is for the good of the client.

   c. Welcome guides and healing Beings of Light to work with you and through you for healing.

   d. Before and during the session focus on the positive, uplifting qualities of that person, seeing them in the perfection. You can visualize the client in a Star of David.

   e. Affirm that no negative or imbalanced energies will be absorbed as you visualize yourself surrounded by white light.

   f. Attune with your healing crystal.

2. **Preparation for the Client:**

   a. Take crystal water, flower, or gem essences.

   b. Hold the appropriate crystals.

3. **Back**

Step 1 — Clearing (See illustration 6c)

   a. The client lies on his or her stomach. Ask the client to visualize a shower of light, relaxing and purifying the body. This process can clear away some "static electricity," opening the way for greater conscious effort. As the drawing out progresses, the client can continue to visualize the clearing of stress from the back.

   b. Scan the back and legs with your hand, about 3 inches or so from the body, for areas of blocked energy. Often there will be blockages in the area of the adrenal glands and shoulders.

   c. **Draw out** from any blocked areas, using a hand-held crystal. Do not draw out from the base of the spine, even if the energy seems blocked there. (You will be placing a crystal there later.) If the client is using the clearing shower visualization, work in the direction of the head to the feet.

d. Check the energy flow in the legs and do any drawing out needed there until all drawing out is completed, and you can feel the energy flowing again.

e. Ask your pendulum to confirm that you have done all the drawing out that is necessary at this time, on the back, checking areas where you spent time.

Step 2 — Infusing Energy for Healing (See Illustration 6d)

a. Place a crystal on the base of the spine, point up toward the head which aids in the realignment of the life force energies. Once the proper positive-negative balance is present at the base of the spine, this message travels up the entire length of the spine.

b. During the infusion process the client can visualize energy and strength revitalizing the body, and other appropriate affirmations for healing.

c. With your hand-held crystal, **infuse** energy into the base of the spine, using counterclockwise rotations, being careful not to overcharge this area.

d. Infuse energy into the adrenals, shoulders, and any other areas from which you cleared blockages.

e. Infuse energy into the buttocks and legs as needed.

f. Infuse energy, using counterclockwise rotations over the base of the neck, being careful not to overcharge this area, visualizing this area receiving sunlight or white light. This is the "basic brain" area which receives energy and sends it to different parts of the body, a "circuit dispatcher area."

g. After hand scanning, check with your pendulum to see if the major areas have received the optimal amount of energy needed at this time. Working with the pendulum will help you fine tune your perception of energy sensations until the time when you don't need to use it. When you are first beginning it can help give you confidence about what you are sensing.

h. Finish evening the flow of energy in the back by making several large counterclockwise sweeps around and above the body.

4. Front

Step 1 – Clearing or Drawing Out (See Illustration 6e)

a. Ask the client to dialogue with their subconscious self and find out what needs releasing, and visualize the release process taking place.

b. Scan the body as you did the back for blocked areas.

c. **Draw out** from any blocked areas using your hand-held crystal until you feel the flow being restored. Check the legs after you check the chakras.

d. Hand scan to check for energy flow, and confirm with your pendulum that the optimal level of drawing out for this time has been done.

Step 2 – Infusing Energy for Healing (See Illustration 6f)

a. Ask the client to visualize healing light, colors, qualities such as courage and joy, and affirmations appropriate to the intuitive guidance received from the subconscious self. Most of all the client can focus on self-acceptance.

b. **Infuse** energy with your hand-held crystal, first in the chakras where you cleared blockages, and then in any other areas where you worked.

c. Check each chakra with counterclockwise rotations beginning with the root chakra to make sure each is optimally balanced. Be careful not to overcharge.

d. Rotate counterclockwise over each leg, checking for optimal energy flow. Confirm with your pendulum that each chakra, and other areas, are in balance.

Step 3 — Spiritual Expansion

a. The client can be encouraged to attune with his or her Higher Self, while in a state of optimal balance. This is a particularly good time to surround the client with a crystal grid.

b. You can conclude the process with any affirming thoughts that reintegrate or reconnect.

Completion

a. Any time you work with clearing energy imbalance or infusing energy for consciousness expansion, you are changing the electro-magnetic fields on a broader scope, heightening the meridians, and changing the energy patterns at each chakra. The process of evening the energies throughout the electromagnetic field is done so that the person can function with a greater sense of balance in earth plane affairs. Several passes need to be made going up through the center of the person's body, holding the crystal parallel with the body. Begin at the highest level above the body where you have worked, moving from the bottom of the feet to the head. Then move to a level approximately halfway between that point and the physical body. Repeat the process in the etheric body several inches above the physical body, and even the energies on that level.

b. The next step is to close the chakras at their optimal level of functioning for grounding and balance. Beginning with the crown chakra, have the client visualize the appropriate chakra closed in a state of perfect balance. Pause at each chakra with the hand-held crystal until the client indicates that the closing is complete, continuing until all the chakras are closed in balance.

c. Give the client time to reorient while lying on the table, and have him or her sit upright for a bit before getting up off the table.

d. Ask the person to stand. If he or she is still feeling dizzy do a standing chakra balance with a crystal.

e. Encourage the person to go outdoors, walk in the grass barefooted, or stand against a tree. You can also ask him or her to visualize a natural setting where they make contact with the earth and their bodies.

f. Give the client crystal water, flower or gem essences to drink.

g. Wash your hands and your hand-held crystal in cold water, visualizing the crystal pure and light-filled, and thank the crystal. Visualize a waterfall cleansing and purifying you, and filling you with light and love. Appreciate your sense of Oneness with All.

In the Appendix the 3-step process is described using additional programmed crystals and grid crystals.

Clockwise and Counterclockwise Rotation of Crystals

The crystal contains two spirals of energy flow, one that moves clockwise within the crystal's internal structure, and the other moving counterclockwise outside the crystal. Though each spiral has its identity and pattern, they interconnect at order points as energy moves from the base of the crystal to its termination. **The way you work with the crystal's energies determines which spiral pattern**

predominates. Whenever a crystal is being rotated, what occurs is the unfoldment of a conal pattern that looks like an ice cream cone. If the rotation is clockwise, the energy is moving from the open area at the top of the cone to the tip of the cone, tightening the energy spirals for a pinpoint focus of life force energies to emerge from the crystal's termination, like an upsidedown ice cream cone. When you rotate a crystal counterclockwise the energy moves in widening spiral from the tip of the cone and emerges in a broad focus from the crystal's termination, like an upright cone.

Most of the time we use a counterclockwise rotation with the hand-held crystal to expand the life force energies in a given area. We use a clockwise rotation sometimes in the infusion process to focus or concentrate the energies of particular programmed crystals. With practice and experience you can sense the different energies produced by clockwise and counterclockwise rotations and decide which rotation suits your purposes.

Further Comments on Healing

Although it is not absolutely essential, a person's trust and willingness to work with you are most helpful. However, if you find that healing energies that are flowing through you are backing up into your fingers, palms, and wrists, this is an indication that the person on some level is choosing at that moment in time to block the flow of vital life energies. When this happens, you have a responsibility to tell the person that it is not possible for you to do anything more for them at this time, and end the session. You must also release any judgmental attitudes about yourself as a channel, or any other negative thoughts related to the experience.

Planetary Healing

A way to deepen our own kinship with all of life is to work with planetary healing. For some crystals this is a way they would specifically like to be used.

To attune to the earth you can take a crystal with you, in your receiving hand as you walk in the woods, and you may feel more deeply the qualities of joy and balance in other living things. Crystals may be left in the ground, points upright, to amplify the earth energies of a particular spot, or you can make a grid at a high energy spot for healing the earth.

When working with a group for planetary healing you can each hold a crystal in your sending hand and focus power through love from your heart and your third eye through the crystal. In this manner you can clear thought pollution in and around the planet, or focus your awareness on infusing light and love for the earth and for humanity. Another way we've worked with crystals is to place them on a world map on areas of need, and focus peace and love. Crystals can also be placed on power spots on the map and their energies amplified.

"For we are all crystals of light and bearers of change. I bring light to your world, your purpose is to bring light to your world also."

A Crystal's Highest Purpose

Every physical phenomenon including humanity, rocks, ocean waves, clouds, each cell or molecule in fact, has an individual consciousness that evolves towards fulfillment of its pattern of growth, in harmony with all of nature. That is one reason why you can see and sense each crystal's energy as unique.

"As the human kingdom grows through life's experiences and through changes of physical vehicles, I too am evolving, for I was created from the same spark of energy as was the human kingdom. I retain knowledge and store within my being just as the human kingdom stores memory also. You see, my capacity for storing knowledge is infinitely greater than that of the human kingdom because the human kingdom has chosen to perceive itself as more limited in different ways. Creative expression to me is a vitally important aspect of my work and important at this time, for I am a catalyst to help pull the human kingdom out of its limits, to see a greater reality, to enable humanity to tap into the far reaches of the infinite cosmos . . ."

We can learn much about unconditional love and other qualities such as patience and trust by attuning with nature's kingdoms.

"I have the ability to instill confidence and courage to all who choose to work with me, for where there is even a seed of those qualities, I have the capacity to expand them within you to their highest ultimate form. Know that it is impossible to hate or fear when you have come into pure connection with me, for I am a channel of pure unconditional love and light for the human kingdom as well as all other kingdoms. (That is why my energies are so well received by the plant kingdoms.) I can enable you to speak with pure truth, with clarity and understanding in all situations and experiences that unfold in life . . ."

Each crystal has a higher purpose to serve which can be ascertained by sitting receptively with the crystal and attuning with it, or by using a pendulum. There are categories of crystals mentioned in other books which can be helpful in finding out more about a crystal's highest purpose. However you can limit the wisdom a crystal can teach you by applying a set of characteristics or descriptions to crystals. Here are some questions that can help you receive intuitive guidance about a crystal's purpose.

1. Is your highest function to restore harmony and balance on the physical, emotional, or mental levels of my being? (healing)

    a. Can you be placed on the physical body?

    b. Are you to work with clearing negative thoughts?

2. Is your highest function to expand the light within my higher spiritual levels? (meditation)

3. Is your highest purpose related to planetary healing?

4. Is it for your highest good to be used for devic communication or other interdimensional communication?

5. Do you have stored symbols or other knowledge inside you, to be accessed receptively?

6. Is it for your highest good to be used in a technological capacity or in a grid system as a transmitter?

Above all it is important to remember that any time you work with a crystal to help you grow spiritually and in service to others, you are fulfilling both your own higher purpose and that of the crystal.

"I am as much a part of you as you are a part of ɪne. Together we have the ability to alter the course of energies that are presently unfolding on the planet. I bring freedom to all relationships, to all beings. Be free now and co-create for the highest good for all forms of life."

REFERENCES AND BIBLIOGRAPHY

Alper, the Reverend Dr. Frank. *Exploring Atlantis, Vols. I and II.* Phoenix, Az: Arizona Metaphysical Society, 3639 East Clarendon Rd., 1982.

Baer, Randall N., and Vicki B. *Windows of Light.* New York: Harper and Row Publishers, Inc., 1984.

Burke, George. *Magnetic Therapy.* Oklahoma City, Ok.: Saint George Press, 1980.

Lantieri, Linda and Elaine Seiler. *Quartz Crystal, A Gift From the Earth.* Northampton, Ma.: Resource Management Ltd., P.O. Box 749, 1985.

Logan, Elizabeth A. *Crystal Cosmos Network Directory.* Winnepeg, Manitoba, Canada R3C 4A6: Crystal Cosmos Network, Box 2386, 1986.

Nielson, Greg and Joseph Polansky. *Pendulum Power.* New York: Warner Books, 1977.

Raphaell, Katrina. *Crystal Enlightenment.* New York: Aurora Press, 1985.

Small, Jacqueline, *Transformers, the Therapists of the Future,* Marina del Ray, Ca.: DeVorss and Company, Box 550, 1982.

Walker, Dale. *The Crystal Book.* Sunol, Ca.: The Crystal Company, 1983.

APPENDIX

Steps in Healing — Level 2

This description includes the use of the 12 point grid and programmed crystals as well as a hand-held crystal, a crystal for the base of the spine, and crystals for the client to hold, to amplify the energy flows.

1. **Preparation for Healing:**

   a. Take crystal water, flower, or gem essences.

   b. Connect any grids you are using and amplify these crystals with counterclockwise rotations.

   c. Center yourself and affirm that your work is for the good of the client.

   d. Welcome guides and healing Beings of Light to work with you and through you for healing.

   e. Before and during the session focus on the positive, uplifting qualities of that person, seeing them in their perfection. You can visualize the client in a Star of David.

   f. Affirm that no negative or imbalanced energies will be absorbed as you visualize yourself surrounded by white light.

   g. Attune with your healing crystal.

2. Preparation for the Client:

   a. Take crystal water, flower, or gem essences.

   b. Hold the appropriate crystals.

3. Back

Step 1 — Clearing (See illustration A1 - p. 95)

1. The client lies on his or her stomach. Ask the client to visualize a shower of light, relaxing and purifying the body. This process can clear away some "static electricity," opening the way for greater conscious effort. As the drawing out progresses, the client can continue to visualize the clearing of stress from the back.

2. Scan the back and legs with your hand about 3 inches or so from the body for areas of blocked energy. You can check to see in what layer of the electromagnetic field the blockage begins and work in that layer. Often there will be blockages in the area of the adrenal glands and shoulders.

3. Crystals can be placed in the right hand and at the bottom of the right foot, pointing away fron the body to aid in the drawing out process.

4. Programmed crystals for drawing out can be placed on the adrenal and shoulder areas in grid patterns, or you can use clusters on these areas.

5. Grid crystals pointing away from the body can be placed at the hip and shoulder areas if needed.

6. **Draw out** from any blocked areas using a hand-held crystal. Do not draw out from the base of the spine, even if the energy seems blocked there. (You will be placing a crystal there later.) If the client is using the clearing shower visualization, work in the direction of the head to the feet.

7. Check the energy flow in the legs and do any drawing out needed there until all drawing out is completed and you can feel the energy flowing again.

Step 2 — Infusing Energy for Healing
(See Illustration A2 — p. 97)

1. Place a crystal on the base of the spine, point up toward the head which aids in the realignment of the life force energies. Once the proper positive-negative balance is present at the base of the spine, this message travels up the entire length of the spine.

2. Crystals can also be placed in the left hand and at the bottom of the left foot pointing in toward the body, for increasing energy flow.

3. Place programmed crystals for infusion of specific colors or qualities on any area where you had programmed crystals for drawing out. Turn these crystals in toward the body or up toward the head.

4. Turn any grid crystals you are using toward the body.

5. With your hand-held crystal, **infuse** energy into the base of the spine, using counterclockwise rotations, being careful not to overcharge the area.

6. **Infuse** energy into the adrenals, shoulders, and any other areas from which you cleared blockages.

7. Infuse energy into the buttocks and legs as needed.

8. Infuse energy using counterclockwise rotations over the base of the neck, being careful not to overcharge this area, visualizing this area receiving sunlight or white light. This is the "basic brain" area which receives energy and sends it to different parts of the body, a "circuit dispatcher area."

9. Finish evening the flow of energy in the back by making several large counterclockwise sweeps around and above the body.

4. **Front**

Step 1 — Clearing or Drawing Out
(See Illustration A3 — p. 99)

1. Ask the client to dialogue with their subconscious self and find out what needs releasing, and visualize the release process taking place.

2. Scan the body as you did the back, for blocked areas.

3. Crystals can be placed in the right hand and at the bottom of the right foot, pointing away from the body to aid in the drawing out process.

4. Programmed crystals for drawing out or clusters can be placed on blocked areas in patterns, points out. Find out in what direction the client is moving the energy and point the crystals up or down.

5. Draw out from any blocked areas using a hand-held crystal, until you feel the flow being restored. Check the legs after you check the chakras.

6. Hand scan to check for energy flow.

Step 2 — Infusing Energy for Healing
(See Illustration A4 — p. 101)

1. Ask the client to visualize healing light, colors, qualities such as courage and joy, and affirmations appropriate to the intuitive guidance received from the subconscious self. Most of all the client can focus on self-acceptance.

2. Place a crystal in the left hand and use all twelve grid crystals pointing in toward the body.

3. Place programmed crystals for color, elements, qualities, or consciousness expansion where you used drawing out crystals, points in or up. You do not need to place crystals on areas that are already balanced.

4. Infuse energy with your hand-held crystal, first in the chakras where you cleared blockages, and then in any other areas where you worked. Check each chakra with counterclockwise rotations beginning with the root chakra to make sure each is optimally balanced. Be careful not to overcharge. Finally rotate over each leg.

Step 3 — Spiritual Expansion
(See Illustration A5 — p. 103)

1. The client can be encouraged to attune with his or her Higher Self, while in a state of optimal balance.

2. Programmed crystals for the expansion of each chakra are placed on the body. Use your intuitive guidance to tell you which chakras would benefit from these crystals.

3. If you are using a 12 point grid, the crystals on the left side of the body can be turned parallel to the body, pointing toward the head and those on the right side turned parallel and pointed toward the feet.

4. You can conclude the process with silence, or with any affirming thoughts that reintegrate or reconnect.

5. **Completion** — Same as level 1.

Key for Layout Possibilities

⋂ Star of David grid crystals

🔒 12 Point grid

▮ Hand-held programmed crystals and back crystal

↑ Smaller programmed crystals

Star of David grid has been omitted from illustrations A3, A4, A5.

A1.

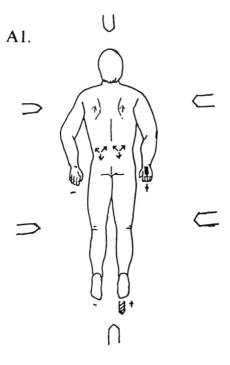

Key for Layout Possibilities

⌂ Star of David grid crystals

🔔 12 Point grid

❚ Hand-held programmed crystals and back crystal

↑ Smaller programmed crystals

Star of David grid has been omitted from illustrations A3, A4, A5.

A2.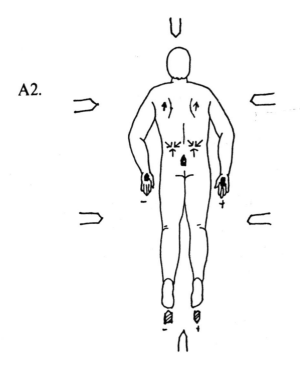

Key for Layout Possibilities

⌂ Star of David grid crystals

⊟ 12 Point grid

▮ Hand-held programmed crystals and back crystal

↑ Smaller programmed crystals

Star of David grid has been omitted from illustrations A3, A4, A5.

A3.

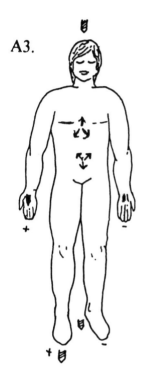

Key for Layout Possibilities

∩ Star of David grid crystals

♬ 12 Point grid

⬆ Hand-held programmed crystals and back crystal

↑ Smaller programmed crystals

Star of David grid has been omitted from illustrations A3, A4, A5.

A4.

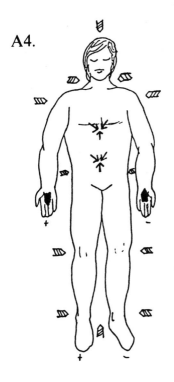

Key for Layout Possibilities

∩ Star of David grid crystals

⊟ 12 Point grid

▮ Hand-held programmed crystals and back crystal

↑ Smaller programmed crystals

Star of David grid has been omitted from illustrations A3, A4, A5.

A5

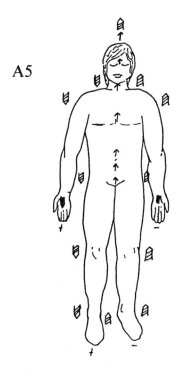

Coleman Publishing
99 Milbar Boulevard
Farmingdale, New York 11735
(516) 293-0383-84